THIS JOURNAL

Belongs To:

wife mom Boss

LoveofLink Publishers

IMPORTANT *Contacts*

NAME & ADDRESS

NAME & ADDRESS

NAME & ADDRESS

NAME & ADDRESS

NAME & ADDRESS

NAME & ADDRESS

NAME & ADDRESS

NAME & ADDRESS

NAME & ADDRESS

NAME & ADDRESS

NAME & ADDRESS

NAME & ADDRESS

Emergency
CONTACT INFORMATION

POLICE DEPARTMENT

FIRE DEPARTMENT

AMBULANCE SERVICES

POISON CONTROL

MOM'S CELL NUMBER

DAD'S CELL NUMBER

SCHOOL

FAMILY DOCTOR

NEIGHBORS

DENTIST

VETERINARIAN

RELATIVES

OTHER

OTHER IMPORTANT INFORMATION

HOUSEHOLD *Contacts*

CONTRACTORS

REPAIR MAN

CLEANING SERVICES

SNOW REMOVAL SERVICES

LANDSCAPING SERVICES

GARBAGE & RECYCLING

BABYSITTERS:

SCHOOLS:

NOTES:

WEBSITES & Passwords

WEBSITE URL:	USERNAME:	PASSWORD:

NOTES:

Family
BIRTHDAYS & ANNIVERSARIES

JANUARY

FEBRUARY

MARCH

APRIL

MAY

JUNE

OTHER

JULY

AUGUST

SEPTEMBER

OCTOBER

NOVEMBER

DECEMBER

OTHER

SCHOOL *Information*

SCHOOL NAME:

PRINCIPAL:

SCHOOL ADDRESS:

PHONE NUMBERS:

BUS DRIVER INFORMATION:

TEACHER & CLASSROOM INFO:

CLASSROOM INFORMATION

CHILD:	TEACHER:	CLASSROOM:	ROOM #:
CHILD:	TEACHER:	CLASSROOM:	ROOM #:
CHILD:	TEACHER:	CLASSROOM:	ROOM #:

MEDICAL *Information*

FAMILY DOCTOR

FAMILY DENTIST

OPTOMETRIST

PEDIATRICIAN

VETERINARIAN

FAMILY INSURANCE INFORMATION

IMPORTANT INFORMATION

ALLERGIES

BLOOD TYPES

WHAT:

WHO:

NAME:

BLOOD TYPE:

TURN *Dreams* INTO *Reality*

TIME FRAME	MY GOALS	STEPS I'LL TAKE
6 MONTHS		
1 YEAR		
2 YEARS		
5 YEARS		

MONTHLY BILL *Tracker*

BILL:

MONTH:	DUE DATE:	BALANCE:	AMOUNT DUE:	AMOUNT PAID:

TOTAL YEARLY COST: $

MONTHLY EXPENSE *Tracker*

BILL:

DATE	EXPENSE	TOTAL	NOTES

TOTAL MONTHLY COST: $

SEASONAL *Cleaning*

WINTER

SPRING

SUMMER

FALL/AUTUMN

SHOPPING *Checklist*

Week by Week
PLANNER

WEEK OF: _____

WEEKLY TASK *Checklist*

MONDAY

- [ ]
- [ ]
- [ ]
- [ ]
- [ ]
- [ ]
- [ ]
- [ ]

TUESDAY

- [ ]
- [ ]
- [ ]
- [ ]
- [ ]
- [ ]
- [ ]
- [ ]

WEDNESDAY

- [ ]
- [ ]
- [ ]
- [ ]
- [ ]
- [ ]
- [ ]
- [ ]

THURSDAY

- [ ]
- [ ]
- [ ]
- [ ]
- [ ]
- [ ]
- [ ]
- [ ]

FRIDAY

- [ ]
- [ ]
- [ ]
- [ ]
- [ ]
- [ ]
- [ ]

SATURDAY

- [ ]
- [ ]
- [ ]
- [ ]
- [ ]
- [ ]
- [ ]

SUNDAY

- [ ]
- [ ]
- [ ]
- [ ]
- [ ]
- [ ]
- [ ]

NOTES & REMINDERS

WEEKLY *Activities*

Monday

Tuesday

Wednesday

Thursday

Friday

Saturday

Sunday

MOM *Goals*

DATE

THINGS I HOPE TO ACCOMPLISH

MY TOP PRIORITIES

Mom's Workout Routine

DATE: _____

ACTIVITY:

TIME: _____   DISTANCE: _____

SETS: _____   REPS: _____

WEIGHT USED: _____   CALORIES BURNED: _____

WATER INTAKE:

WORKOUT ROUTINE

mom fuel

FAMILY MEAL *Planner*

WEEK OF:

CIRCLE DAY: **M:**   **T:**   **W:**   **T:**   **F:**   **S:**   **S:**

BREAKFAST	NOTES

SNACK	NOTES

LUNCH	NOTES

SNACK	NOTES

DINNER/SUPPER	NOTES

GROCERY *Checklist*

Produce

- [ ]
- [ ]
- [ ]
- [ ]
- [ ]
- [ ]
- [ ]
- [ ]
- [ ]
- [ ]
- [ ]
- [ ]

Meats

- [ ]
- [ ]
- [ ]
- [ ]
- [ ]
- [ ]
- [ ]
- [ ]
- [ ]
- [ ]
- [ ]
- [ ]

Dairy

- [ ]
- [ ]
- [ ]
- [ ]
- [ ]
- [ ]
- [ ]
- [ ]
- [ ]
- [ ]
- [ ]
- [ ]

Frozen

- [ ]
- [ ]
- [ ]
- [ ]
- [ ]
- [ ]
- [ ]
- [ ]
- [ ]

Desserts

- [ ]
- [ ]
- [ ]
- [ ]
- [ ]
- [ ]
- [ ]
- [ ]
- [ ]

Misc.

- [ ]
- [ ]
- [ ]
- [ ]
- [ ]
- [ ]
- [ ]
- [ ]
- [ ]

FROM MOM'S *Kitchen*

Recipe

PREP TIME:	BAKE TIME:	SERVES:

Ingredients

Directions

HOUSEWORK *Checklist*

CLEANING SUPPLY INVENTORY

WEEKLY CLEANING TO DO LIST

ORGANIZATION PRIORITIES

REFRIGERATOR INVENTORY
Tracker

ITEMS	QUANTITY	NOTES

FREEZER INVENTORY *Tracker*

ITEMS	QUANTITY	NOTES

CABINET INVENTORY *Tracker*

ITEMS	QUANTITY	NOTES

PANTRY INVENTORY *Tracker*

ITEMS	QUANTITY	NOTES

CLEANING SUPPLIES *Inventory*

ITEMS	QUANTITY	NOTES

FAMILY SAVINGS *Tracker*

WE'RE SAVING FOR:

AMOUNT
NEEDED:

OUR GOAL DATE:

DEPOSIT TRACKER

AMOUNT DEPOSITED: **DATE DEPOSITED:**

$

$

$

$

$

$

$

$

$

KIDS CHORE *Chart*

NAME:

CHORE:	M:	T:	W:	T:	F:	S:	S:

Week by Week

PLANNER

WEEK OF: _____

WEEKLY TASK *Checklist*

MONDAY

☐
☐
☐
☐
☐
☐
☐
☐

TUESDAY

☐
☐
☐
☐
☐
☐
☐
☐

WEDNESDAY

☐
☐
☐
☐
☐
☐
☐
☐

THURSDAY

☐
☐
☐
☐
☐
☐
☐

FRIDAY

☐
☐
☐
☐
☐
☐
☐

SATURDAY

☐
☐
☐
☐
☐
☐
☐

SUNDAY

☐
☐
☐
☐
☐
☐
☐

NOTES & REMINDERS

WEEKLY *Activities*

Monday

Tuesday

Wednesday

Thursday

Friday

Saturday

Sunday

PERSONAL *Goals*

WEEKLY TO DO LIST: M   T   W   T   F   S   S

MOM'S DAILY *Journal*

DATE:

WHAT I DID TODAY

HIGHLIGHT OF THE DAY

Mom's Workout Routine

DATE:

ACTIVITY:

TIME:

DISTANCE:

SETS:

REPS:

WEIGHT USED:

CALORIES BURNED:

WATER INTAKE:

WORKOUT ROUTINE

mom fuel

FAMILY MEAL *Planner*

WEEK OF: _____

CIRCLE DAY: **M:**   **T:**   **W:**   **T:**   **F:**   **S:**   **S:**

BREAKFAST	NOTES

SNACK	NOTES

LUNCH	NOTES

SNACK	NOTES

DINNER/SUPPER	NOTES

GROCERY *Checklist*

Produce

Meats

Dairy

Frozen

Desserts

Misc.

FROM MOM'S *Kitchen*

Recipe

PREP TIME:	BAKE TIME:	SERVES:

Ingredients

Directions

HOUSEWORK *Checklist*

CLEANING SUPPLY INVENTORY

- ☐
- ☐
- ☐
- ☐
- ☐
- ☐
- ☐
- ☐

- ☐
- ☐
- ☐
- ☐
- ☐
- ☐
- ☐
- ☐

WEEKLY CLEANING TO DO LIST

- ☐
- ☐
- ☐
- ☐
- ☐
- ☐
- ☐
- ☐

- ☐
- ☐
- ☐
- ☐
- ☐
- ☐
- ☐

ORGANIZATION PRIORITIES

- ☐
- ☐
- ☐
- ☐
- ☐
- ☐
- ☐

- ☐
- ☐
- ☐
- ☐
- ☐
- ☐

REFRIGERATOR INVENTORY
Tracker

ITEMS	QUANTITY	NOTES

FREEZER INVENTORY *Tracker*

ITEMS	QUANTITY	NOTES

CABINET INVENTORY *Tracker*

ITEMS	QUANTITY	NOTES

PANTRY INVENTORY *Tracker*

ITEMS	QUANTITY	NOTES

CLEANING SUPPLIES
Inventory

ITEMS	QUANTITY	NOTES

FAMILY SAVINGS *Tracker*

WE'RE SAVING FOR:

AMOUNT
NEEDED:

OUR GOAL DATE:

DEPOSIT TRACKER

AMOUNT DEPOSITED: **DATE DEPOSITED:**

$

$

$

$

$

$

$

$

$

$

KIDS CHORE *Chart*

NAME:

CHORE:	M:	T:	W:	T:	F:	S:	S:

Week by Week
PLANNER

WEEK OF:

WEEKLY TASK *Checklist*

MONDAY

- [ ]
- [ ]
- [ ]
- [ ]
- [ ]
- [ ]
- [ ]
- [ ]

TUESDAY

- [ ]
- [ ]
- [ ]
- [ ]
- [ ]
- [ ]
- [ ]
- [ ]

WEDNESDAY

- [ ]
- [ ]
- [ ]
- [ ]
- [ ]
- [ ]
- [ ]
- [ ]

THURSDAY

- [ ]
- [ ]
- [ ]
- [ ]
- [ ]
- [ ]
- [ ]
- [ ]

FRIDAY

- [ ]
- [ ]
- [ ]
- [ ]
- [ ]
- [ ]
- [ ]
- [ ]

SATURDAY

- [ ]
- [ ]
- [ ]
- [ ]
- [ ]
- [ ]
- [ ]
- [ ]

SUNDAY

- [ ]
- [ ]
- [ ]
- [ ]
- [ ]
- [ ]
- [ ]
- [ ]

NOTES & REMINDERS

WEEKLY *Activities*

Monday

Tuesday

Wednesday

Thursday

Friday

Saturday

Sunday

MOM'S DAILY *Journal*

DATE:

WHAT I DID TODAY

HIGHLIGHT OF THE DAY

MY PERSONAL *Goals*

THIS WEEK'S GOALS

THIS MONTH'S GOALS

STEPS TO GET IT DONE

Mom's Workout Routine

DATE: _____

ACTIVITY:

TIME:	DISTANCE:
SETS:	REPS:
WEIGHT USED:	CALORIES BURNED:

WATER INTAKE:

WORKOUT ROUTINE

mom fuel

FAMILY MEAL *Planner*

WEEK OF:

CIRCLE DAY:	**M:**	**T:**	**W:**	**T:**	**F:**	**S:**	**S:**

BREAKFAST	NOTES

SNACK	NOTES

LUNCH	NOTES

SNACK	NOTES

DINNER/SUPPER	NOTES

GROCERY *Checklist*

Produce

- [ ] _____
- [ ] _____
- [ ] _____
- [ ] _____
- [ ] _____
- [ ] _____
- [ ] _____
- [ ] _____
- [ ] _____
- [ ] _____
- [ ] _____
- [ ] _____

Meats

- [ ] _____
- [ ] _____
- [ ] _____
- [ ] _____
- [ ] _____
- [ ] _____
- [ ] _____
- [ ] _____
- [ ] _____
- [ ] _____
- [ ] _____
- [ ] _____

Dairy

- [ ] _____
- [ ] _____
- [ ] _____
- [ ] _____
- [ ] _____
- [ ] _____
- [ ] _____
- [ ] _____
- [ ] _____
- [ ] _____
- [ ] _____
- [ ] _____

Frozen

- [ ] _____
- [ ] _____
- [ ] _____
- [ ] _____
- [ ] _____
- [ ] _____
- [ ] _____
- [ ] _____

Desserts

- [ ] _____
- [ ] _____
- [ ] _____
- [ ] _____
- [ ] _____
- [ ] _____
- [ ] _____
- [ ] _____

Misc.

- [ ] _____
- [ ] _____
- [ ] _____
- [ ] _____
- [ ] _____
- [ ] _____
- [ ] _____
- [ ] _____

FROM MOM'S *Kitchen*

Recipe

PREP TIME:	BAKE TIME:	SERVES:

Ingredients

Directions

HOUSEWORK *Checklist*

CLEANING SUPPLY INVENTORY

- [ ]
- [ ]
- [ ]
- [ ]
- [ ]
- [ ]
- [ ]
- [ ]

- [ ]
- [ ]
- [ ]
- [ ]
- [ ]
- [ ]
- [ ]
- [ ]

WEEKLY CLEANING TO DO LIST

- [ ]
- [ ]
- [ ]
- [ ]
- [ ]
- [ ]
- [ ]
- [ ]

- [ ]
- [ ]
- [ ]
- [ ]
- [ ]
- [ ]
- [ ]
- [ ]

ORGANIZATION PRIORITIES

- [ ]
- [ ]
- [ ]
- [ ]
- [ ]
- [ ]
- [ ]

- [ ]
- [ ]
- [ ]
- [ ]
- [ ]
- [ ]
- [ ]

REFRIGERATOR INVENTORY
Tracker

ITEMS	QUANTITY	NOTES

FREEZER INVENTORY *Tracker*

ITEMS	QUANTITY	NOTES

CABINET INVENTORY *Tracker*

ITEMS	QUANTITY	NOTES

PANTRY INVENTORY *Tracker*

ITEMS	QUANTITY	NOTES

CLEANING SUPPLIES *Inventory*

ITEMS	QUANTITY	NOTES

FAMILY SAVINGS *Tracker*

WE'RE SAVING FOR:

AMOUNT
NEEDED:

OUR GOAL DATE:

DEPOSIT TRACKER

AMOUNT DEPOSITED: **DATE DEPOSITED:**

$

$

$

$

$

$

$

$

$

$

KIDS CHORE *Chart*

NAME:

CHORE:	M:	T:	W:	T:	F:	S:	S:

Week by Week
PLANNER

WEEK OF: _____

WEEKLY TASK *Checklist*

MONDAY

- ☐
- ☐
- ☐
- ☐
- ☐
- ☐
- ☐
- ☐

TUESDAY

- ☐
- ☐
- ☐
- ☐
- ☐
- ☐
- ☐
- ☐

WEDNESDAY

- ☐
- ☐
- ☐
- ☐
- ☐
- ☐
- ☐
- ☐

THURSDAY

- ☐
- ☐
- ☐
- ☐
- ☐
- ☐
- ☐
- ☐

FRIDAY

- ☐
- ☐
- ☐
- ☐
- ☐
- ☐
- ☐
- ☐

SATURDAY

- ☐
- ☐
- ☐
- ☐
- ☐
- ☐
- ☐

SUNDAY

- ☐
- ☐
- ☐
- ☐
- ☐
- ☐
- ☐
- ☐

NOTES & REMINDERS

WEEKLY *Activities*

Monday

Tuesday

Wednesday

Thursday

Friday

Saturday

Sunday

MOM *Goals*

DATE

THINGS I HOPE TO ACCOMPLISH

MY TOP PRIORITIES

Mom's Workout Routine

DATE:

ACTIVITY:

TIME:

DISTANCE:

SETS:

REPS:

WEIGHT USED:

CALORIES BURNED:

WATER INTAKE:

WORKOUT ROUTINE

mom fuel

FAMILY MEAL *Planner*

WEEK OF: _____

CIRCLE DAY:	M:	T:	W:	T:	F:	S:	S:

BREAKFAST	NOTES

SNACK	NOTES

LUNCH	NOTES

SNACK	NOTES

DINNER/SUPPER	NOTES

GROCERY *Checklist*

Produce

- [ ] _____
- [ ] _____
- [ ] _____
- [ ] _____
- [ ] _____
- [ ] _____
- [ ] _____
- [ ] _____
- [ ] _____
- [ ] _____

Meats

- [ ] _____
- [ ] _____
- [ ] _____
- [ ] _____
- [ ] _____
- [ ] _____
- [ ] _____
- [ ] _____
- [ ] _____
- [ ] _____

Dairy

- [ ] _____
- [ ] _____
- [ ] _____
- [ ] _____
- [ ] _____
- [ ] _____
- [ ] _____
- [ ] _____
- [ ] _____
- [ ] _____

Frozen

- [ ] _____
- [ ] _____
- [ ] _____
- [ ] _____
- [ ] _____
- [ ] _____
- [ ] _____
- [ ] _____

Desserts

- [ ] _____
- [ ] _____
- [ ] _____
- [ ] _____
- [ ] _____
- [ ] _____
- [ ] _____
- [ ] _____

Misc.

- [ ] _____
- [ ] _____
- [ ] _____
- [ ] _____
- [ ] _____
- [ ] _____
- [ ] _____
- [ ] _____

FROM MOM'S *Kitchen*

Recipe

PREP TIME:	BAKE TIME:	SERVES:

Ingredients

Directions

HOUSEWORK *Checklist*

CLEANING SUPPLY INVENTORY

- [ ]
- [ ]
- [ ]
- [ ]
- [ ]
- [ ]
- [ ]
- [ ]

- [ ]
- [ ]
- [ ]
- [ ]
- [ ]
- [ ]
- [ ]
- [ ]

WEEKLY CLEANING TO DO LIST

- [ ]
- [ ]
- [ ]
- [ ]
- [ ]
- [ ]
- [ ]
- [ ]

- [ ]
- [ ]
- [ ]
- [ ]
- [ ]
- [ ]
- [ ]
- [ ]

ORGANIZATION PRIORITIES

- [ ]
- [ ]
- [ ]
- [ ]
- [ ]
- [ ]
- [ ]

- [ ]
- [ ]
- [ ]
- [ ]
- [ ]
- [ ]
- [ ]

REFRIGERATOR INVENTORY
Tracker

ITEMS	QUANTITY	NOTES

FREEZER INVENTORY *Tracker*

ITEMS	QUANTITY	NOTES

CABINET INVENTORY
Tracker

ITEMS	QUANTITY	NOTES

PANTRY INVENTORY *Tracker*

ITEMS	QUANTITY	NOTES

CLEANING SUPPLIES *Inventory*

ITEMS	QUANTITY	NOTES

FAMILY SAVINGS *Tracker*

WE'RE SAVING FOR:

AMOUNT
NEEDED:

OUR GOAL DATE:

DEPOSIT TRACKER

AMOUNT DEPOSITED: **DATE DEPOSITED:**

$

$

$

$

$

$

$

$

$

$

KIDS CHORE *Chart*

NAME:

CHORE:	M:	T:	W:	T:	F:	S:	S:

Week by Week

PLANNER

WEEK OF:

WEEKLY TASK *Checklist*

MONDAY

- [ ]
- [ ]
- [ ]
- [ ]
- [ ]
- [ ]
- [ ]
- [ ]

TUESDAY

- [ ]
- [ ]
- [ ]
- [ ]
- [ ]
- [ ]
- [ ]
- [ ]

WEDNESDAY

- [ ]
- [ ]
- [ ]
- [ ]
- [ ]
- [ ]

THURSDAY

- [ ]
- [ ]
- [ ]
- [ ]
- [ ]
- [ ]
- [ ]
- [ ]

FRIDAY

- [ ]
- [ ]
- [ ]
- [ ]
- [ ]
- [ ]
- [ ]

SATURDAY

- [ ]
- [ ]
- [ ]
- [ ]
- [ ]
- [ ]

SUNDAY

- [ ]
- [ ]
- [ ]
- [ ]
- [ ]
- [ ]
- [ ]
- [ ]

NOTES & REMINDERS

WEEKLY *Activities*

Monday

Tuesday

Wednesday

Thursday

Friday

Saturday

Sunday

PERSONAL *Goals*

WEEKLY TO DO LIST: M   T   W   T   F   S   S

Mom's Workout Routine

DATE: _____

ACTIVITY:

TIME: _____

DISTANCE: _____

SETS: _____

REPS: _____

WEIGHT USED: _____

CALORIES BURNED: _____

WATER INTAKE:

WORKOUT ROUTINE

mom fuel

FAMILY MEAL *Planner*

WEEK OF:

CIRCLE DAY:	M:	T:	W:	T:	F:	S:	S:

BREAKFAST	NOTES

SNACK	NOTES

LUNCH	NOTES

SNACK	NOTES

DINNER/SUPPER	NOTES

GROCERY *Checklist*

Produce

Meats

Dairy

Frozen

Desserts

Misc.

FROM MOM'S *Kitchen*

Recipe

PREP TIME:	BAKE TIME:	SERVES:

Ingredients

Directions

HOUSEWORK *Checklist*

CLEANING SUPPLY INVENTORY

- ☐
- ☐
- ☐
- ☐
- ☐
- ☐
- ☐
- ☐

- ☐
- ☐
- ☐
- ☐
- ☐
- ☐
- ☐
- ☐

WEEKLY CLEANING TO DO LIST

- ☐
- ☐
- ☐
- ☐
- ☐
- ☐
- ☐
- ☐

- ☐
- ☐
- ☐
- ☐
- ☐
- ☐
- ☐
- ☐

ORGANIZATION PRIORITIES

- ☐
- ☐
- ☐
- ☐
- ☐
- ☐
- ☐

- ☐
- ☐
- ☐
- ☐
- ☐
- ☐
- ☐

REFRIGERATOR INVENTORY
Tracker

ITEMS	QUANTITY	NOTES

FREEZER INVENTORY
Tracker

ITEMS	QUANTITY	NOTES

CABINET INVENTORY *Tracker*

ITEMS	QUANTITY	NOTES

PANTRY INVENTORY *Tracker*

ITEMS	QUANTITY	NOTES

CLEANING SUPPLIES
Inventory

ITEMS	QUANTITY	NOTES

FAMILY SAVINGS *Tracker*

WE'RE SAVING FOR:

AMOUNT
NEEDED:

OUR GOAL DATE:

DEPOSIT TRACKER

AMOUNT DEPOSITED: **DATE DEPOSITED:**

$

$

$

$

$

$

$

$

$

$

KIDS CHORE *Chart*

NAME:

CHORE:	M:	T:	W:	T:	F:	S:	S:

Week by Week

PLANNER

WEEK OF:

WEEKLY TASK *Checklist*

MONDAY

- [ ]
- [ ]
- [ ]
- [ ]
- [ ]
- [ ]
- [ ]
- [ ]

TUESDAY

- [ ]
- [ ]
- [ ]
- [ ]
- [ ]
- [ ]
- [ ]
- [ ]

WEDNESDAY

- [ ]
- [ ]
- [ ]
- [ ]
- [ ]
- [ ]
- [ ]
- [ ]

THURSDAY

- [ ]
- [ ]
- [ ]
- [ ]
- [ ]
- [ ]
- [ ]
- [ ]

FRIDAY

- [ ]
- [ ]
- [ ]
- [ ]
- [ ]
- [ ]
- [ ]
- [ ]

SATURDAY

- [ ]
- [ ]
- [ ]
- [ ]
- [ ]
- [ ]
- [ ]
- [ ]

SUNDAY

- [ ]
- [ ]
- [ ]
- [ ]
- [ ]
- [ ]
- [ ]
- [ ]

NOTES & REMINDERS

WEEKLY *Activities*

Monday

Tuesday

Wednesday

Thursday

Friday

Saturday

Sunday

PERSONAL *Goals*

WEEKLY TO DO LIST: **M T W T F S S**

Mom's Workout Routine

DATE: _____

ACTIVITY:

TIME:	**DISTANCE:**
SETS:	**REPS:**
WEIGHT USED:	**CALORIES BURNED:**

WATER INTAKE:

WORKOUT ROUTINE

mom fuel

FAMILY MEAL *Planner*

WEEK OF:

CIRCLE DAY: **M:** **T:** **W:** **T:** **F:** **S:** **S:**

BREAKFAST	NOTES

SNACK	NOTES

LUNCH	NOTES

SNACK	NOTES

DINNER/SUPPER	NOTES

GROCERY *Checklist*

Produce

Meats

Dairy

Frozen

Desserts

Misc.

FROM MOM'S *Kitchen*

Recipe

PREP TIME:	BAKE TIME:	SERVES:

Ingredients

Directions

HOUSEWORK *Checklist*

CLEANING SUPPLY INVENTORY

- [ ]
- [ ]
- [ ]
- [ ]
- [ ]
- [ ]
- [ ]
- [ ]

- [ ]
- [ ]
- [ ]
- [ ]
- [ ]
- [ ]
- [ ]
- [ ]

WEEKLY CLEANING TO DO LIST

- [ ]
- [ ]
- [ ]
- [ ]
- [ ]
- [ ]
- [ ]
- [ ]

- [ ]
- [ ]
- [ ]
- [ ]
- [ ]
- [ ]

ORGANIZATION PRIORITIES

- [ ]
- [ ]
- [ ]
- [ ]
- [ ]
- [ ]
- [ ]

- [ ]
- [ ]
- [ ]
- [ ]
- [ ]
- [ ]

REFRIGERATOR INVENTORY
Tracker

ITEMS	QUANTITY	NOTES

FREEZER INVENTORY *Tracker*

ITEMS	QUANTITY	NOTES

CABINET INVENTORY
Tracker

ITEMS	QUANTITY	NOTES

PANTRY INVENTORY *Tracker*

ITEMS	QUANTITY	NOTES

CLEANING SUPPLIES *Inventory*

ITEMS	QUANTITY	NOTES

FAMILY SAVINGS *Tracker*

WE'RE SAVING FOR:

AMOUNT
NEEDED:

OUR GOAL DATE:

DEPOSIT TRACKER

AMOUNT DEPOSITED:	DATE DEPOSITED:
$	
$	
$	
$	
$	
$	
$	
$	
$	

KIDS CHORE *Chart*

NAME:

CHORE:	M:	T:	W:	T:	F:	S:	S:

Week by Week
PLANNER

WEEK OF:

WEEKLY TASK *Checklist*

MONDAY

- [ ]
- [ ]
- [ ]
- [ ]
- [ ]
- [ ]
- [ ]
- [ ]

TUESDAY

- [ ]
- [ ]
- [ ]
- [ ]
- [ ]
- [ ]
- [ ]
- [ ]

WEDNESDAY

- [ ]
- [ ]
- [ ]
- [ ]
- [ ]
- [ ]
- [ ]

THURSDAY

- [ ]
- [ ]
- [ ]
- [ ]
- [ ]
- [ ]
- [ ]
- [ ]

FRIDAY

- [ ]
- [ ]
- [ ]
- [ ]
- [ ]
- [ ]
- [ ]

SATURDAY

- [ ]
- [ ]
- [ ]
- [ ]
- [ ]
- [ ]

SUNDAY

- [ ]
- [ ]
- [ ]
- [ ]
- [ ]
- [ ]
- [ ]
- [ ]

NOTES & REMINDERS

WEEKLY *Activities*

Monday

Tuesday

Wednesday

Thursday

Friday

Saturday

Sunday

MOM *Goals*

DATE

THINGS I HOPE TO ACCOMPLISH

MY TOP PRIORITIES

Mom's Workout Routine

DATE: _____

ACTIVITY:

TIME: _____   DISTANCE: _____

SETS: _____   REPS: _____

WEIGHT USED: _____   CALORIES BURNED: _____

WATER INTAKE:

WORKOUT ROUTINE

mom fuel

FAMILY MEAL *Planner*

WEEK OF:

CIRCLE DAY:	M:	T:	W:	T:	F:	S:	S:

BREAKFAST	NOTES

SNACK	NOTES

LUNCH	NOTES

SNACK	NOTES

DINNER/SUPPER	NOTES

GROCERY *Checklist*

Produce

- [ ] _____
- [ ] _____
- [ ] _____
- [ ] _____
- [ ] _____
- [ ] _____
- [ ] _____
- [ ] _____
- [ ] _____
- [ ] _____

Meats

- [ ] _____
- [ ] _____
- [ ] _____
- [ ] _____
- [ ] _____
- [ ] _____
- [ ] _____
- [ ] _____
- [ ] _____
- [ ] _____

Dairy

- [ ] _____
- [ ] _____
- [ ] _____
- [ ] _____
- [ ] _____
- [ ] _____
- [ ] _____
- [ ] _____
- [ ] _____
- [ ] _____

Frozen

- [ ] _____
- [ ] _____
- [ ] _____
- [ ] _____
- [ ] _____
- [ ] _____
- [ ] _____

Desserts

- [ ] _____
- [ ] _____
- [ ] _____
- [ ] _____
- [ ] _____
- [ ] _____
- [ ] _____

Misc.

- [ ] _____
- [ ] _____
- [ ] _____
- [ ] _____
- [ ] _____
- [ ] _____
- [ ] _____

FROM MOM'S *Kitchen*

Recipe

PREP TIME:	BAKE TIME:	SERVES:

Ingredients

Directions

HOUSEWORK *Checklist*

CLEANING SUPPLY INVENTORY

WEEKLY CLEANING TO DO LIST

ORGANIZATION PRIORITIES

REFRIGERATOR INVENTORY
Tracker

ITEMS	QUANTITY	NOTES

FREEZER INVENTORY *Tracker*

ITEMS	QUANTITY	NOTES

CABINET INVENTORY *Tracker*

ITEMS	QUANTITY	NOTES

CLEANING SUPPLIES
Inventory

ITEMS	QUANTITY	NOTES

FAMILY SAVINGS *Tracker*

WE'RE SAVING FOR:

AMOUNT
NEEDED:

OUR GOAL DATE:

DEPOSIT TRACKER

AMOUNT DEPOSITED: **DATE DEPOSITED:**

$

$

$

$

$

$

$

$

$

$

KIDS CHORE *Chart*

NAME:

CHORE:	M:	T:	W:	T:	F:	S:	S:

Week by Week

PLANNER

WEEK OF:

WEEKLY TASK *Checklist*

MONDAY

- [ ]
- [ ]
- [ ]
- [ ]
- [ ]
- [ ]
- [ ]

TUESDAY

- [ ]
- [ ]
- [ ]
- [ ]
- [ ]
- [ ]
- [ ]
- [ ]

WEDNESDAY

- [ ]
- [ ]
- [ ]
- [ ]
- [ ]
- [ ]
- [ ]

THURSDAY

- [ ]
- [ ]
- [ ]
- [ ]
- [ ]
- [ ]
- [ ]

FRIDAY

- [ ]
- [ ]
- [ ]
- [ ]
- [ ]
- [ ]
- [ ]

SATURDAY

- [ ]
- [ ]
- [ ]
- [ ]
- [ ]
- [ ]
- [ ]

SUNDAY

- [ ]
- [ ]
- [ ]
- [ ]
- [ ]
- [ ]
- [ ]

NOTES & REMINDERS

WEEKLY *Activities*

Monday

Tuesday

Wednesday

Thursday

Friday

Saturday

Sunday

PERSONAL *Goals*

WEEKLY TO DO LIST:

	M	T	W	T	F	S	S
	○	○	○	○	○	○	○
	○	○	○	○	○	○	○
	○	○	○	○	○	○	○
	○	○	○	○	○	○	○
	○	○	○	○	○	○	○
	○	○	○	○	○	○	○
	○	○	○	○	○	○	○
	○	○	○	○	○	○	○
	○	○	○	○	○	○	○
	○	○	○	○	○	○	○
	○	○	○	○	○	○	○
	○	○	○	○	○	○	○
	○	○	○	○	○	○	○
	○	○	○	○	○	○	○
	○	○	○	○	○	○	○

Mom's Workout Routine

DATE:

ACTIVITY:

TIME:

DISTANCE:

SETS:

REPS:

WEIGHT USED:

CALORIES BURNED:

WATER INTAKE:

WORKOUT ROUTINE

mom fuel

FAMILY MEAL *Planner*

WEEK OF: _____

CIRCLE DAY:	M:	T:	W:	T:	F:	S:	S:

BREAKFAST

NOTES

SNACK

NOTES

LUNCH

NOTES

SNACK

NOTES

DINNER/SUPPER

NOTES

GROCERY *Checklist*

Produce

Meats

Dairy

Frozen

Desserts

Misc.

FROM MOM'S *Kitchen*

Recipe

PREP TIME:	BAKE TIME:	SERVES:

Ingredients

Directions

HOUSEWORK *Checklist*

CLEANING SUPPLY INVENTORY

WEEKLY CLEANING TO DO LIST

ORGANIZATION PRIORITIES

FAMILY SAVINGS *Tracker*

WE'RE SAVING FOR:

AMOUNT
NEEDED:

OUR GOAL DATE:

DEPOSIT TRACKER

AMOUNT DEPOSITED: **DATE DEPOSITED:**

$

$

$

$

$

$

$

$

$

$

Week by Week

PLANNER

WEEK OF:

WEEKLY TASK *Checklist*

MONDAY
- [ ]
- [ ]
- [ ]
- [ ]
- [ ]
- [ ]
- [ ]
- [ ]

TUESDAY
- [ ]
- [ ]
- [ ]
- [ ]
- [ ]
- [ ]
- [ ]
- [ ]

WEDNESDAY
- [ ]
- [ ]
- [ ]
- [ ]
- [ ]
- [ ]
- [ ]
- [ ]

THURSDAY
- [ ]
- [ ]
- [ ]
- [ ]
- [ ]
- [ ]
- [ ]
- [ ]

FRIDAY
- [ ]
- [ ]
- [ ]
- [ ]
- [ ]
- [ ]
- [ ]
- [ ]

SATURDAY
- [ ]
- [ ]
- [ ]
- [ ]
- [ ]
- [ ]
- [ ]
- [ ]

SUNDAY
- [ ]
- [ ]
- [ ]
- [ ]
- [ ]
- [ ]
- [ ]
- [ ]

NOTES & REMINDERS

WEEKLY *Activities*

Monday

Tuesday

Wednesday

Thursday

Friday

Saturday

Sunday

MOM *Goals*

DATE

THINGS I HOPE TO ACCOMPLISH

MY TOP PRIORITIES

Mom's Workout Routine

DATE:

ACTIVITY:

TIME:

DISTANCE:

SETS:

REPS:

WEIGHT USED:

CALORIES BURNED:

WATER INTAKE:

WORKOUT ROUTINE

mom fuel

FAMILY MEAL *Planner*

WEEK OF: _____

CIRCLE DAY:	M:	T:	W:	T:	F:	S:	S:

BREAKFAST	NOTES

SNACK	NOTES

LUNCH	NOTES

SNACK	NOTES

DINNER/SUPPER	NOTES

GROCERY *Checklist*

Produce

Meats

Dairy

Frozen

Desserts

Misc.

SHOPPING *Checklist*

FROM MOM'S *Kitchen*

Recipe

PREP TIME:	BAKE TIME:	SERVES:

Ingredients

Directions

HOUSEWORK *Checklist*

CLEANING SUPPLY INVENTORY

WEEKLY CLEANING TO DO LIST

ORGANIZATION PRIORITIES

REFRIGERATOR INVENTORY
Tracker

ITEMS	QUANTITY	NOTES

FAMILY SAVINGS *Tracker*

WE'RE SAVING FOR:

AMOUNT
NEEDED:

OUR GOAL DATE:

DEPOSIT TRACKER

AMOUNT DEPOSITED: **DATE DEPOSITED:**

$

$

$

$

$

$

$

$

$

$

KIDS CHORE *Chart*

NAME:

CHORE:	M:	T:	W:	T:	F:	S:	S:

Made in United States
Orlando, FL
22 January 2024

42778924R00083